I0472006

Praise for *Awaken:*
Reveal your beliefs. Shape your culture. Propel your business.

"*Awaken* gives us a fresh perspective on today's business beliefs, while challenging us to lead what we believe. Finding a simple yet, inspiring tool that empowers entrepreneurs, leaders and team members to become the change they desire is rare. Awaken fits the bill introducing a new book format that involves the reader in their own process of transformation."

-- Chris LoCurto, Vice President of The Lampo Group

"Business moves at such a breakneck pace today that, if we're not careful, we can get carried away and lose sight of our core guiding beliefs. *Awaken* not only reminds us to pause for a moment to think about what we believe, but it also gives us a framework to further define those beliefs and bring them to life in our businesses.

Scott is one of my 'go-to guys' for business wisdom and counsel, and I know that after you read this book, he'll be one of yours, too!"

-- Shawn Ellis, Founder of The Speakers Group

"*Awaken* is a refreshing process that helped me discover my true core beliefs that have now become the foundational building blocks of my business. This book has helped me awaken a renewed enthusiasm for the work I do and helped me focus on the reasons I work so hard to make my business successful. *Awaken* could revolutionize the way businesses operate."

-- Dennis Martin, actor, acting coach, author,
owner of Prompter Talent

"*Awaken* asks the right questions to help a person determine the "why" within their business. The unique thought book format empowers us to discover our true beliefs and act on them.

Experiencing Scott within a business group setting for the past year and a half, *Awaken* amplifies his philosophy in business and in life which is to be true to your beliefs."

-- Paul Geisen, owner of Ergonomic Wellness, LLC.

Beliefs drive behaviors.
Behaviors yield negative or positive consequences.
Cultures are shaped by behaviors.

Here are a few beliefs that have changed the world:

Ferdinand Magellan's…
proved the earth was round.

Galileo Galilei's beliefs…
discovered our solar system.

Thomas Edison's beliefs…
gave us the light bulb.

The Wright Brother's beliefs…
gave us flight.

Henry Ford's beliefs…
gave us an automobile for the masses.

Gandhi's beliefs…
transformed India.

Martin Luther King's beliefs…
solidified the equal rights movement.

John F. Kennedy's beliefs…
challenged man to land on the moon.

Sir Timothy Berners-Lee's beliefs…
gave us the world wide web.

Mark Zuckerberg's beliefs…
gave us Facebook.

What do you believe?

Published by:

Nashville, TN

Author: Scott Cutcher
Logo & Cover Design: Scott Cutcher & Steven Lowry
Layout & Design: Steven Lowry
Editor: Monica Ayers
Published by: GamePlan, LLC.
Printed & Distributed by: Lulu.com

To order *Awaken* in bulk, connect with us at:
www.awakenmybeliefs.com

If you wish to learn more about our other
products/services connect with us at:
www.gameplanmentoring.com

This book is dedicated to the amazing women in our lives, Cindy Cutcher and Kelly Lowry.

Your belief in us has made this journey towards our vision possible.

Table of Contents

Purpose of Awaken

What do you believe and why?

If you have never defined, articulated, or confirmed your beliefs, then your actions are being governed by someone else's beliefs. Whether it was a parent, friend, spouse, or colleague who shared, imposed, or illustrated their beliefs to you, someone has influenced your behavior through their beliefs. Understanding your beliefs and discerning which ones are truly yours is the first step in becoming who you were designed to be and influence the culture around you.

Everyone has that moment when an experience shatters a previous perception and a new belief begins to form. I had one of those experiences in my early thirties, and it made me question every belief I ever had. The revelation? Most of my beliefs weren't truly mine, and they were sabotaging my ability to achieve my dreams. Frustrated by this revelation, I went on a quest to discover who I truly was at my core. Simply, what I believed and why I believed it. The realization was that my values and my beliefs didn't match up. This disconnect played havoc in my life, especially in my professional life. I continually felt that I was falling short of my goals.

I began looking for a process that would challenge me to not only think deeply but also solidify what I truly believed. It was all there in the pages among the philosophical ramblings of some brilliant thought leaders, and after three years of introspection I knew without a doubt what I believed. Like a newly ordained minister, I now freely share my beliefs with my friends, family, and clients when prompted (even sometimes without prompting). I discovered that simply stating what you believe is the best way to find out what others believe. Under scrutiny, imposed beliefs will waiver, but true beliefs stand firm.

Could getting people to understand what they believe really be that easy? Tested and proven, the concept for *Awaken* was born.

We are currently experiencing fundamental shifts in human behaviors, especially consumer behaviors which influence the markets. Entrepreneurs, small businesses, and other organizations are struggling to adjust to these fundamental shifts often reacting to them instead of navigating them.

A business revolution has begun with young and intuitive organizations leading the way by innovating through an understanding of what they believe, why they believe what they believe, and aligning what they believe with their daily actions. This is creating dynamic business cultures that are revolutionizing the way we do business. Who is leading this movement? Companies such as Zappos, Threadless, Google, and Facebook, to mention a few.

Knowledge is potential power. True power, however, only exists when knowledge is put into action. Many books contain great information, but they lack the ability to easily transform that information into usable, implementable data. Thus, the concept of a "thought book" was born.

So, what is a "thought book?"

A "thought book" presents a synopsis of a subject matter while utilizing a reflective process that makes a series of statements. Statements are then followed by a series of questions, causing you to think about each statement and journal your thoughts.

The purpose of this "thought book" is to awaken your own beliefs about the four core areas of business and create from these beliefs a set of values that will guide your actions. We believe that the four core areas of business from which all other areas are developed are: Self, Environment, Opportunities, and Connection. Whether your beliefs align with ours or not, the question is, are your beliefs truly yours or someone else's? Are your beliefs empowering a culture of growth or sabotaging the current culture?

> *"What we can or cannot do, what we consider possible or impossible, is rarely a function of our true capability. It is more likely a function of our beliefs about who we are."*
> *- Anthony Robbins*

Awaken is formatted to spur deep thought. We state what we believe and challenge you to agree or disagree with each belief. Space is provided to journal your thoughts. We will also examine three different success stories and how their beliefs played a major role in their accomplishments. First, we will look at an example of beliefs used from a self-governance point of view. Second, we'll look at an example of beliefs transferred from a leader to an organization that influenced a culture. Finally, we'll examine beliefs compiled by a collective group and utilized to form a culture.

We believe that the sharing of knowledge is the truest expression of humble power. This makes you stronger and empowers others. *Awaken* puts this belief into action by providing you with the chance to collaborate via our Facebook page. There you can engage us, along with others, in an honest dialog about beliefs and how these beliefs will influence business in the next decade.

Whether you are an individual, a startup, a department, or a corporation, we have outlined how to get the most out of this experience. Pick the outline that best suits your situation.

Personal: Simply experience *Awaken* by yourself. Utilize the format to provoke thought, awaken your inner dialog, and validate your beliefs to better live according to them.

Partner: Same as personal, except, you will partner up with a colleague, a friend, or a family member and experience *Awaken* together. Schedule regular meetings to discuss any revelations. Use the simple outline in the conclusion section to create your personal manifesto(s).

Startups: Involve your partner(s), a fellow entrepreneur, colleague, friend or family member and experience *Awaken* together. Utilize the format to provoke thought, awaken your inner dialog, and validate your beliefs while meeting regularly to discuss any revelations. Using the simple outline in the conclusion section, create a manifesto to use in developing your company culture.

Department: Use as a team building exercise and experience *Awaken* together. Utilize the format to provoke thought, awaken your inner dialog, and validate your beliefs while meeting regularly to discuss any revelations. Using the simple outline in the conclusion section, create a manifesto to use in developing your departmental culture that will empower the company vision.

Corporate: Use as a team building exercise and experience *Awaken* together as a company. Utilize the format to provoke thought, awaken your inner dialog, and validate your beliefs while meeting regularly to discuss any revelations. Using the simple outline in the conclusion section, create a manifesto to use in developing a corporate culture that empowers the company vision.

Caution: Don't rush the process. One belief a day is optimal to allow honest, inner reflection and create engaging dialog.

Are you ready to awaken your true beliefs
and capture your full potential?

Awaken Yourself
philosophical beliefs

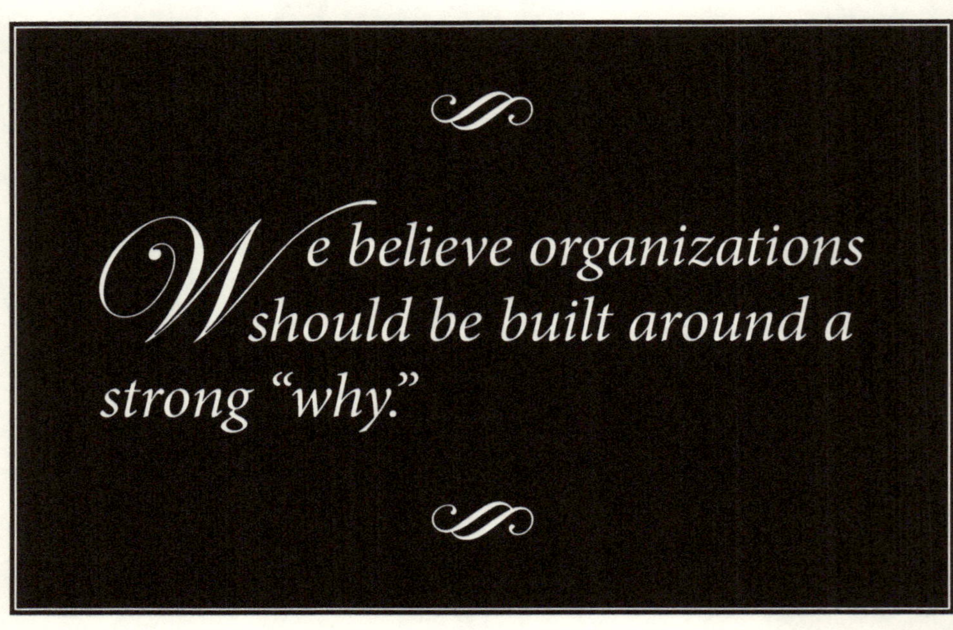
We believe organizations should be built around a strong "why."

Journal your initial thoughts below:

Belief Journal

1. If you do not agree, create a belief statement using your own words. If you do agree, feel free to put this belief into your own words.

2. Did this belief come from your own experiences or from some else's beliefs? Explain.

3. What values will guide your actions in living out this belief?

"For those who believe, no proof is necessary.
For those who don't believe, no proof is possible."
- Stuart Chase

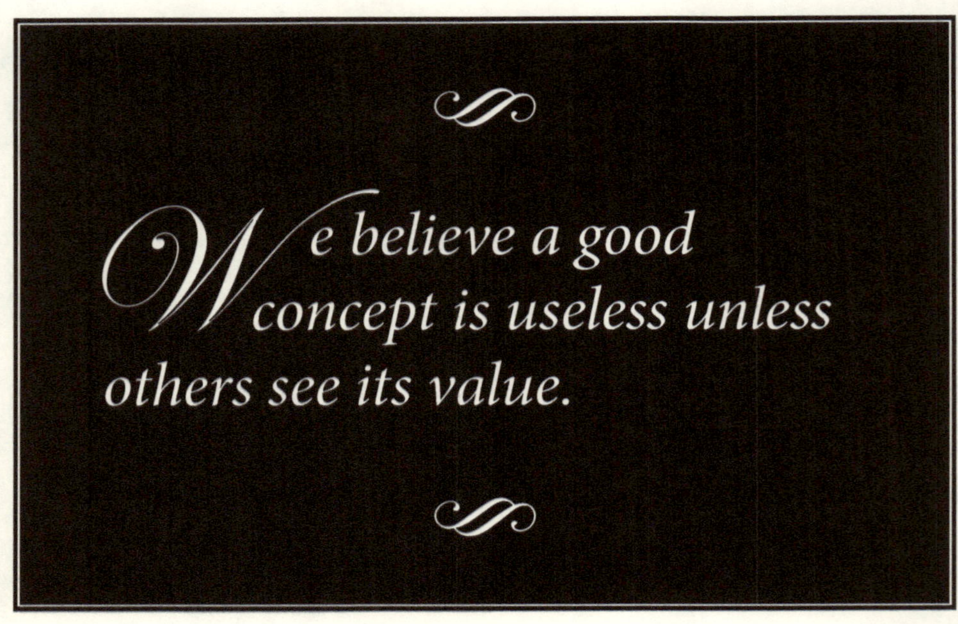
We believe a good concept is useless unless others see its value.

Journal your initial thoughts below:

BELIEF JOURNAL

1. **If you do not agree, create a belief statement using your own words. If you do agree, feel free to put this belief into your own words.**

2. **Did this belief come from your own experiences or from some else's beliefs? Explain.**

3. **What values will guide your actions in living out this belief?**

"Men often become what they believe themselves to be. If I believe I cannot do something, it makes me incapable of doing it. But when I believe I can, then I acquire the ability to do it even if I didn't have it in the beginning."
- Mahatma Gandhi

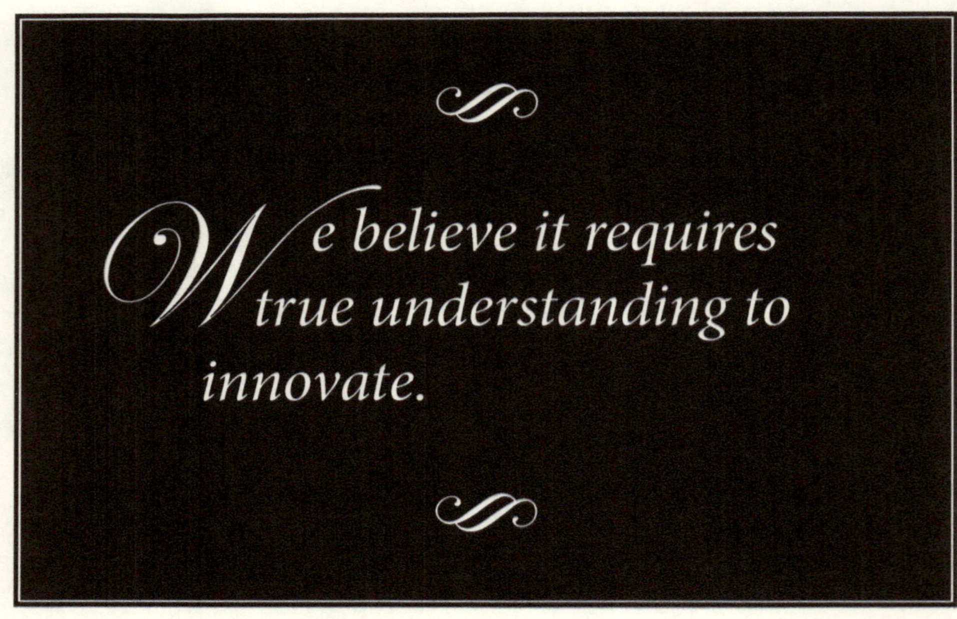

We believe it requires true understanding to innovate.

Journal your initial thoughts below:

Belief Journal

1. **If you do not agree, create a belief statement using your own words. If you do agree, feel free to put this belief into your own words.**

2. **Did this belief come from your own experiences or from some else's beliefs? Explain.**

3. **What values will guide your actions in living out this belief?**

"One life is all we have and we live it as we believe in living it. But to sacrifice what you are and to live without belief, that is a fate more terrible than dying."
- Joan of Arc

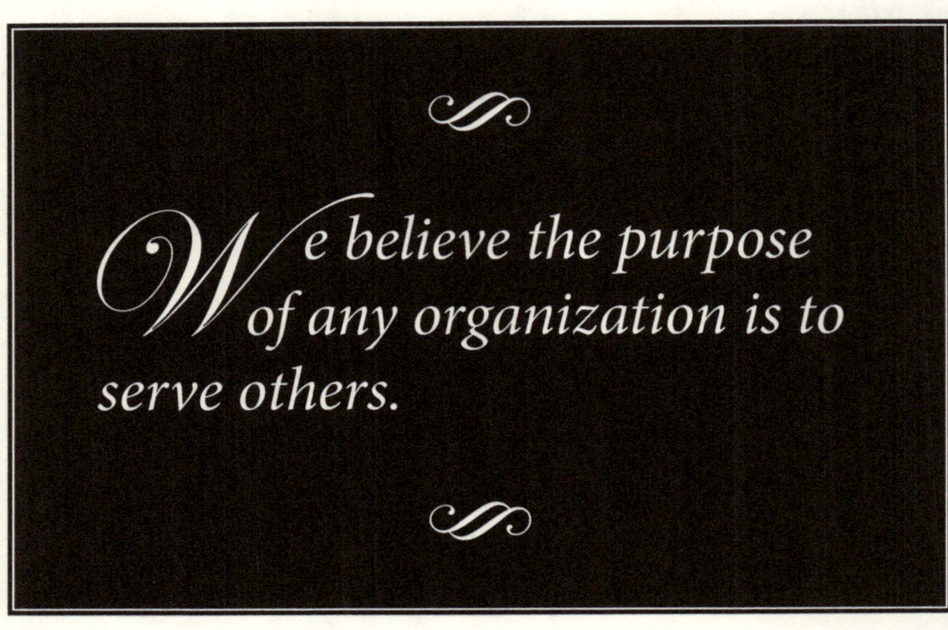
We believe the purpose of any organization is to serve others.

Journal your initial thoughts below:

Belief Journal

1. If you do not agree, create a belief statement using your own words. If you do agree, feel free to put this belief into your own words.

2. Did this belief come from your own experiences or from some else's beliefs? Explain.

3. What values will guide your actions in living out this belief?

"Live your beliefs and you can turn the world around."
- Henry David Thoreau

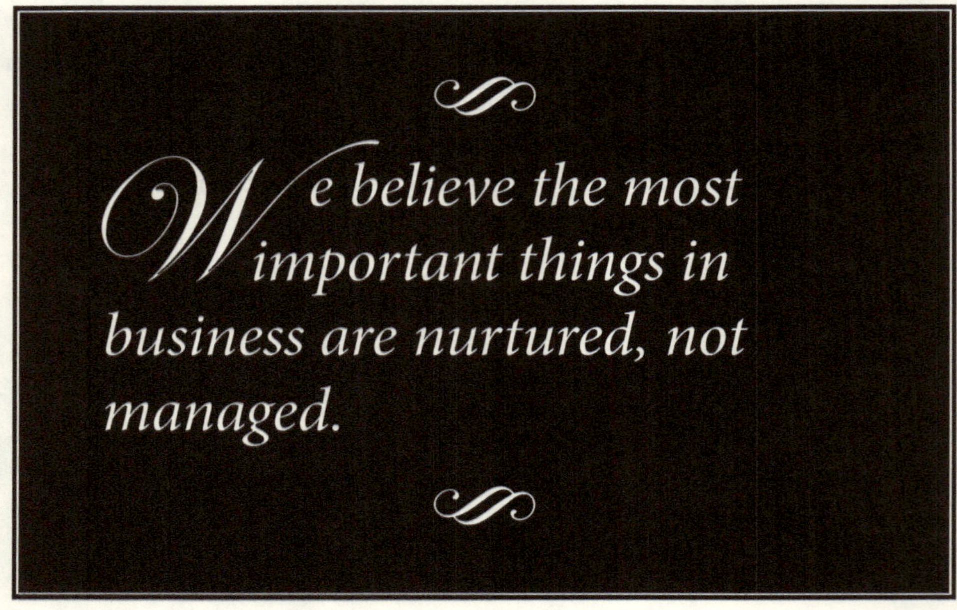

We believe the most important things in business are nurtured, not managed.

Journal your initial thoughts below:

Belief Journal

1. If you do not agree, create a belief statement using your own words. If you do agree, feel free to put this belief into your own words.

2. Did this belief come from your own experiences or from some else's beliefs? Explain.

3. What values will guide your actions in living out this belief?

"The outer conditions of a person's life will always be found to reflect their inner beliefs."
- James Allen

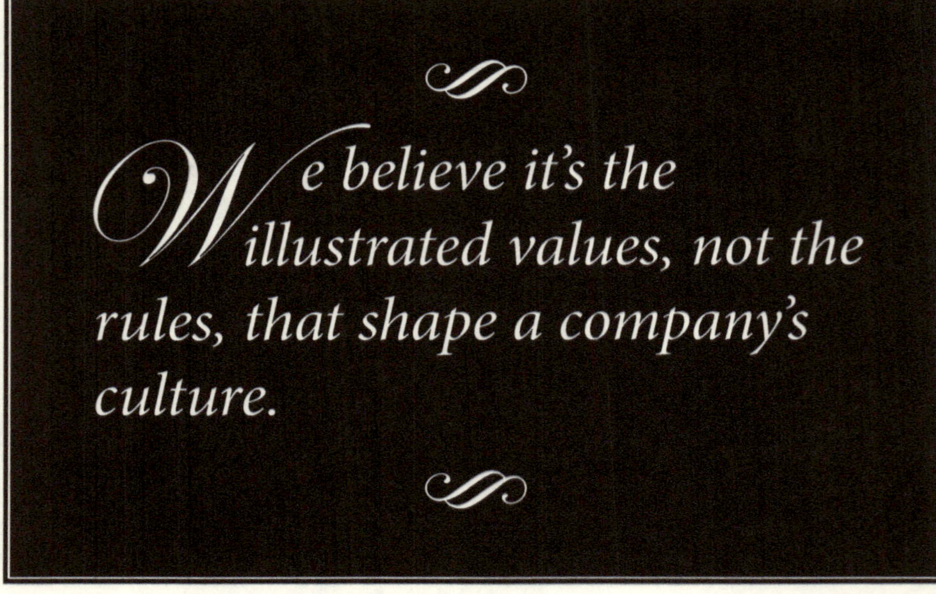

We believe it's the illustrated values, not the rules, that shape a company's culture.

Journal your initial thoughts below:

Belief Journal

1. If you do not agree, create a belief statement using your own words. If you do agree, feel free to put this belief into your own words.

2. Did this belief come from your own experiences or from some else's beliefs? Explain.

3. What values will guide your actions in living out this belief?

"One must marry one's feelings to one's beliefs and ideas. That is probably the only way to achieve a measure of harmony in one's life."
- Napoleon Hill

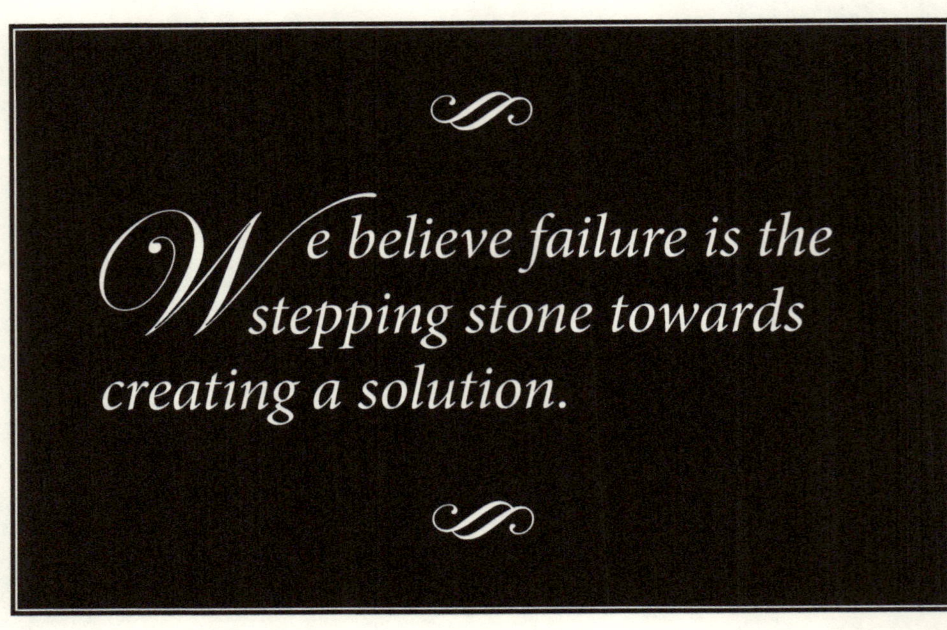
We believe failure is the stepping stone towards creating a solution.

Journal your initial thoughts below:

Belief Journal

1. If you do not agree, create a belief statement using your own words. If you do agree, feel free to put this belief into your own words.

2. Did this belief come from your own experiences or from some else's beliefs? Explain.

3. What values will guide your actions in living out this belief?

"What distinguishes the majority of men from the few is their inability to act according to their beliefs."
- John Stuart Mill

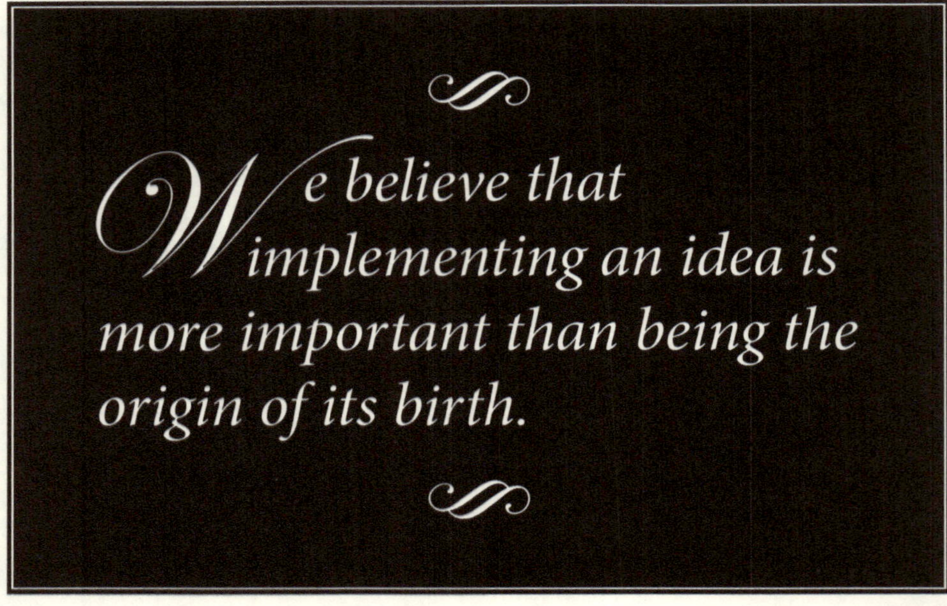

We believe that implementing an idea is more important than being the origin of its birth.

Journal your initial thoughts below:

Belief Journal

1. If you do not agree, create a belief statement using your own words. If you do agree, feel free to put this belief into your own words.

2. Did this belief come from your own experiences or from some else's beliefs? Explain.

3. What values will guide your actions in living out this belief?

"We are what we believe we are."
- Benjamin N. Cardozo

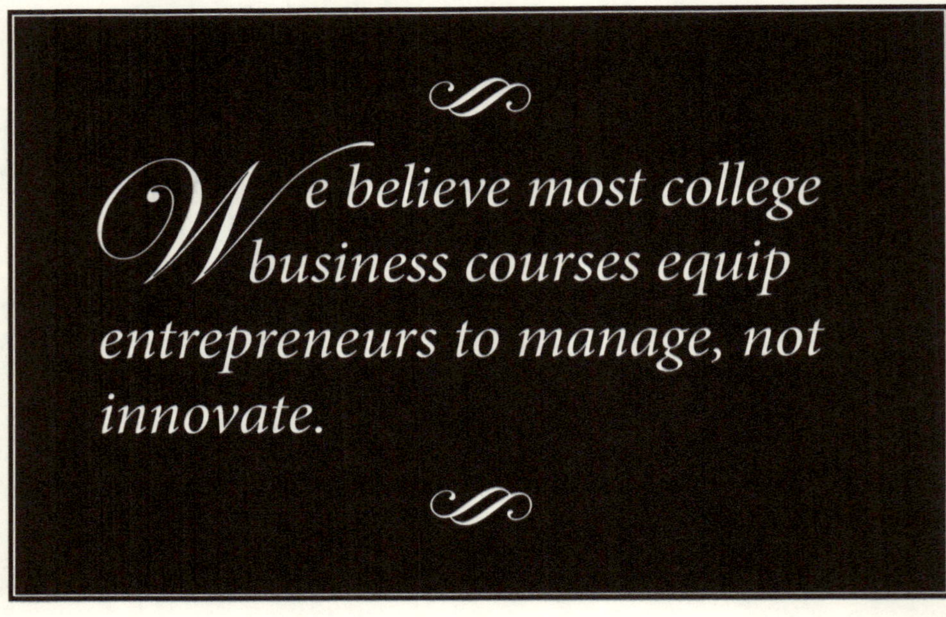

We believe most college business courses equip entrepreneurs to manage, not innovate.

Journal your initial thoughts below:

Belief Journal

1. If you do not agree, create a belief statement using your own words. If you do agree, feel free to put this belief into your own words.

2. Did this belief come from your own experiences or from some else's beliefs? Explain.

3. What values will guide your actions in living out this belief?

"Our belief at the beginning of a doubtful undertaking is the one thing that assures the successful outcome of any venture."
- William James

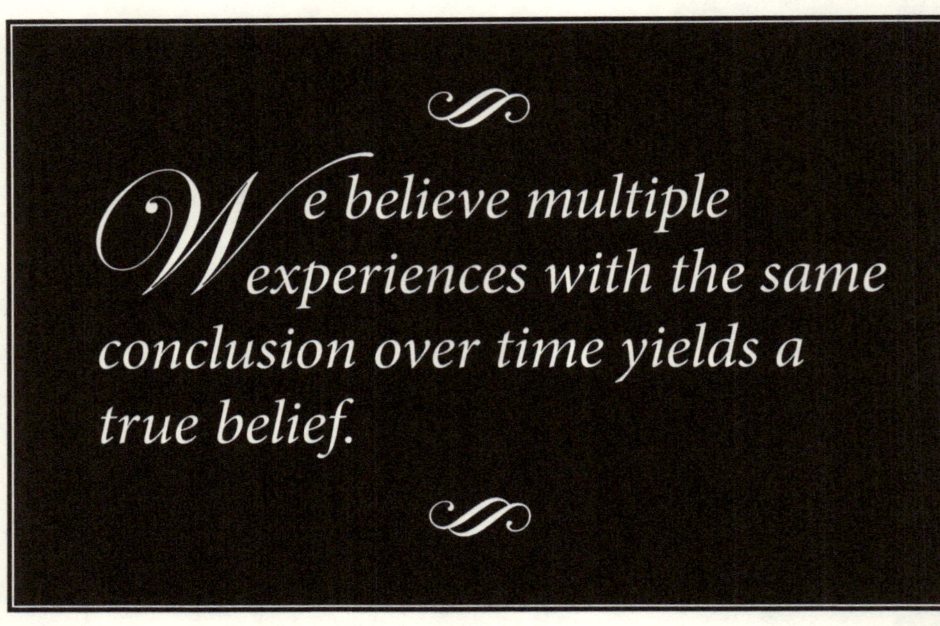

We believe multiple experiences with the same conclusion over time yields a true belief.

Journal your initial thoughts below:

Belief Journal

1. If you do not agree, create a belief statement using your own words. If you do agree, feel free to put this belief into your own words.

2. Did this belief come from your own experiences or from some else's beliefs? Explain.

3. What values will guide your actions in living out this belief?

"A belief is not merely an idea the mind possesses; it is an idea that possesses the mind."
- Robert Oxton Bol

BENJAMIN FRANKLIN

Benjamin Franklin is a shining example of self-governing beliefs. Franklin used his beliefs to guide his actions through thirteen virtues, which he had written down in a notebook. He placed one virtue on each page, and he kept track of his ability to practice them by reviewing his progress every evening. Franklin would focus on one virtue a week to improve upon, cycling through all thirteen four times a year. What's ironic is discipline was not listed as a virtue, yet an abundance of it was required for daily follow through. I believe Franklin not only focused on the virtues that he held in high regard but also those that did not come naturally. As far as we know, Franklin was only focused on the use of these virtues in his own life. It would stand to reason, however, that his actions also influenced those around him.

Benjamin Franklin is known as a renaissance man, accomplishing much in his lifetime due to the diverse roles he played. Many attribute his success to the virtues he pledged to live by. According to his autobiography, the following are the virtues by which he strived to live. He started when he was just twenty years old.

13 Virtues

1. Temperance: Eat not to dullness; drink not to elevation.
2. Silence: Speak not but what may benefit others or yourself; avoid trifling conversation.
3. Order: Let all your things have their places; let each part of your business have its time.
4. Resolution: Resolve to perform what you ought; perform without fail what you resolve.
5. Frugality: Make no expense but to do good to others or yourself; i.e., waste nothing.
6. Industry: Lose no time; be always employ'd in something useful; cut off all unnecessary actions.
7. Sincerity: Use no hurtful deceit; think innocently and justly, and, if you speak, speak accordingly.
8. Justice: Wrong none by doing injuries, or omitting the benefits that are your duty.
9. Moderation: Avoid extremes; forbear resenting injuries so much as you think they deserve.
10. Cleanliness: Tolerate no uncleanliness in body, clothes, or habitation.
11. Tranquility: Be not disturbed at trifles, or at accidents common or unavoidable.
12. Chastity: Rarely use venery but for health or offspring, never to dullness, weakness, or the injury of your own or another's peace or reputation.
13. Humility: Imitate Jesus and Socrates.

Accomplishments

The following is a timeline of the roles he played and accomplishments that have been attributed to him. Do you see how Franklin's virtues may have served him in obtaining these accomplishments?

1722	Begins writing a series of letters under the pseudonym "Silence Dogood."
1723	Runs away to Philadelphia, finding work in the printing shop of Samuel Keimer.
1724	Sails for England, continuing his training as a printer.
1726	Returns to Philadelphia and works as clerk, bookkeeper, and shopkeeper for Thomas Denham.
1727	Forms the Junto, a club for "self-improvement, study, mutual aid, and conviviality."
1728	Co-founds printing shop with Hugh Meredith.
1729	Purchases The Pennsylvania Gazette, which over the course of 19 years becomes renowned for its humor, originality, and strong influence on public opinion.
1730	Named official printer for Pennsylvania.
1731	Establishes The Library Company of Philadelphia, the first lending library in America.
	Launches one of the colonies' first printing franchises in South Carolina.
1732	Issues the first edition of Poor Richard's Almanac, an instant best-seller that quickly becomes the most popular almanac in the colonies.
1736	Helps found the Union Fire Company, which organizes and trains teams of firemen.
1737	Begins service as postmaster of Philadelphia, continuing until 1753.

1740-41 Designs the Pennsylvania fireplace, now known as the Franklin stove.

1743 Publishes A Proposal for Promoting Useful Knowledge, leading to the formation of the American Philosophical Society.

1748 Retires from the printing business at the age of forty-two.

1750 Designs the lightning rod to divert lightning from buildings during thunderstorms.

1751 Experiments and Observations on Electricity, a collection of Franklin's letters about his electrical experiments, published in London.

Co-founded the Pennsylvania Hospital, the colonies' first public hospital.

Founded the Philadelphia Contributionship, the colonies' first property insurance company.

1752 Performs legendary kite and key experiment, confirming his theory that electricity existed in thunderclouds in the form of lightning.

1753 Awarded the Royal Society of London's Copley Medal for work in electricity.

Appointed joint deputy postmaster general of North America.

Awarded honorary degrees from Harvard and Yale.

1754 Drafts the Albany Plan of Union, urging the colonies to form a united defense against threats from the French and their Native American allies.

Publishes in The Pennsylvania Gazette the "Join, or Die" cartoon, America's first symbol of the united colonies.

1756 Awarded an honorary Master of Arts degree from William and Mary College.

1757 Appointed colonial agent to London.

1758 A Way to Wealth, a collection of Franklin's Poor Richard's writings is published.

1759 Awarded an honorary Doctor of Law degree from the University of St. Andrews, Scotland.

1762 Invents the glass armonica.

Awarded an honorary doctorate degree from Oxford University, England.

1766 Elected to Royal Society of Sciences.

1769 Elected president of the American Philosophical Society.

1771 Begins writing his autobiography.

1775 Elected the Pennsylvania delegate to the Second Continental Congress.

1776 Serves on the committee to draft the Declaration of Independence.

Appointed commissioner to the court of France.

1778 Helps negotiate and signs the Treaty of Amity and Commerce between America and France, securing critical support from the French in the form of loans, military supplies, and troops.

1783	Helps negotiate and signs Treaty of Paris, officially ending the Revolutionary War.
1785	Moves back to Philadelphia after his years of service in France.
1787	Elected president of the Pennsylvania Society for Promoting the Abolition of Slavery. Serves as delegate to the Constitutional Convention.

Looking at the roles Benjamin Franklin played throughout his life, I believe it is fair to say his virtues highly influenced the level of success he experienced in each role. How much more could you accomplish by understanding, articulating, and acting on your beliefs?

Awaken Your Environment

market beliefs

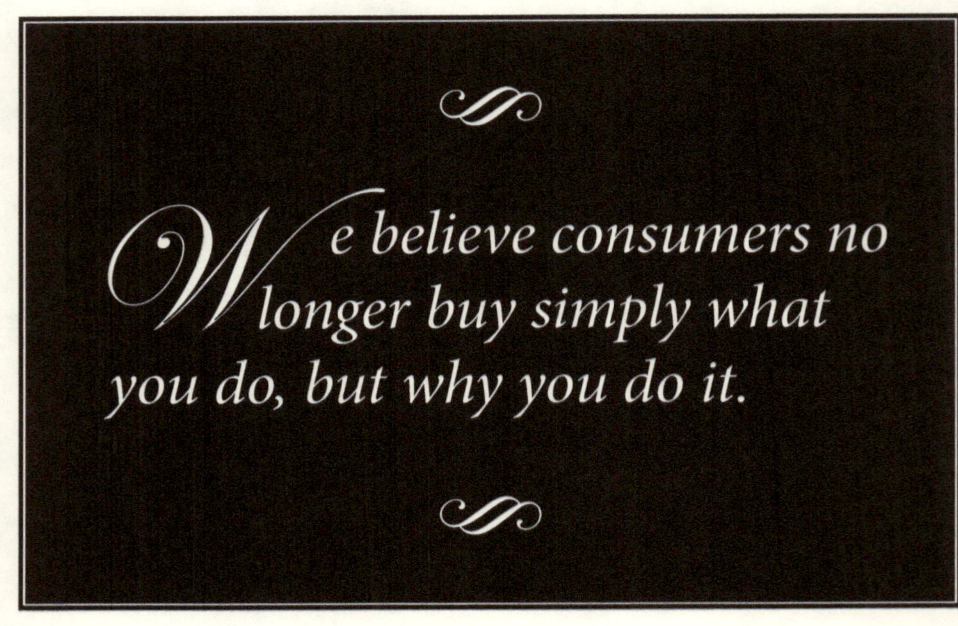

We believe consumers no longer buy simply what you do, but why you do it.

Journal your initial thoughts below:

Belief Journal

1. If you do not agree, create a belief statement using your own words. If you do agree, feel free to put this belief into your own words.

2. Did this belief come from your own experiences or from some else's beliefs? Explain.

3. What values will guide your actions in living out this belief?

"The outer conditions of a person's life will always be found to reflect their inner beliefs."
- James Lane Allen

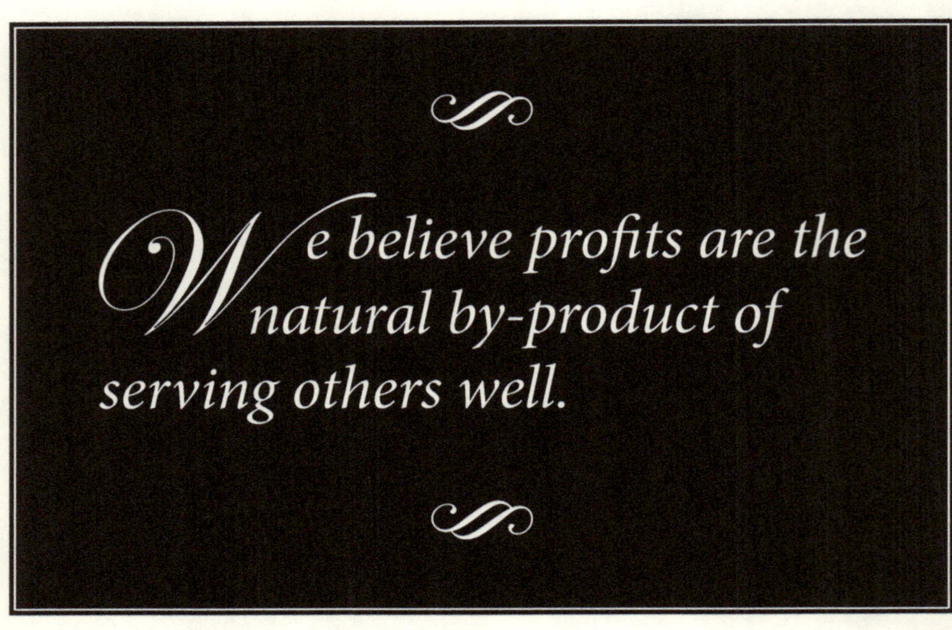

Journal your initial thoughts below:

Belief Journal

1. **If you do not agree, create a belief statement using your own words. If you do agree, feel free to put this belief into your own words.**

2. **Did this belief come from your own experiences or from some else's beliefs? Explain.**

3. **What values will guide your actions in living out this belief?**

"What we need is not the will to believe, but the wish to find out."
- Bertrand Russell

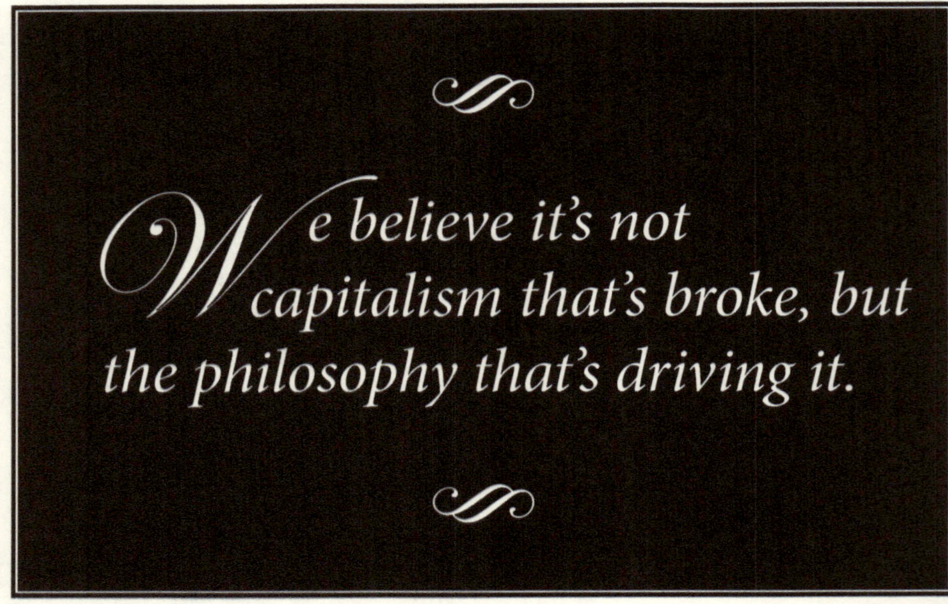
We believe it's not capitalism that's broke, but the philosophy that's driving it.

Journal your initial thoughts below:

Belief Journal

1. **If you do not agree, create a belief statement using your own words. If you do agree, feel free to put this belief into your own words.**

2. **Did this belief come from your own experiences or from some else's beliefs? Explain.**

3. **What values will guide your actions in living out this belief?**

"It's the repetition of affirmations that leads to belief.
And once that belief becomes a deep conviction, things begin to happen."
- Claude M. Bristol

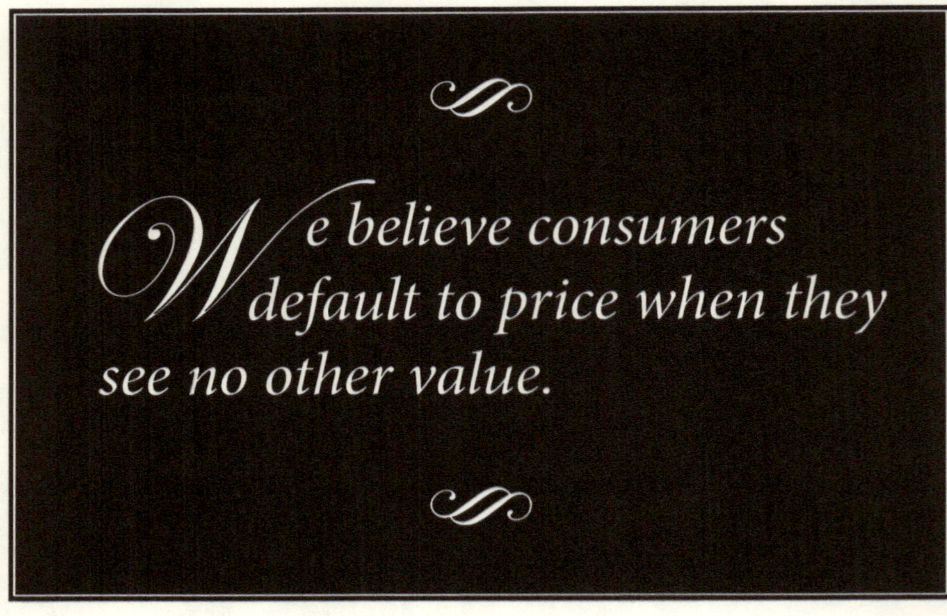

We believe consumers default to price when they see no other value.

Journal your initial thoughts below:

Belief Journal

1. If you do not agree, create a belief statement using your own words. If you do agree, feel free to put this belief into your own words.

2. Did this belief come from your own experiences or from some else's beliefs? Explain.

3. What values will guide your actions in living out this belief?

"Your belief determines your action and your action determines your results, but first you have to believe."
- Mark Victor Hansen

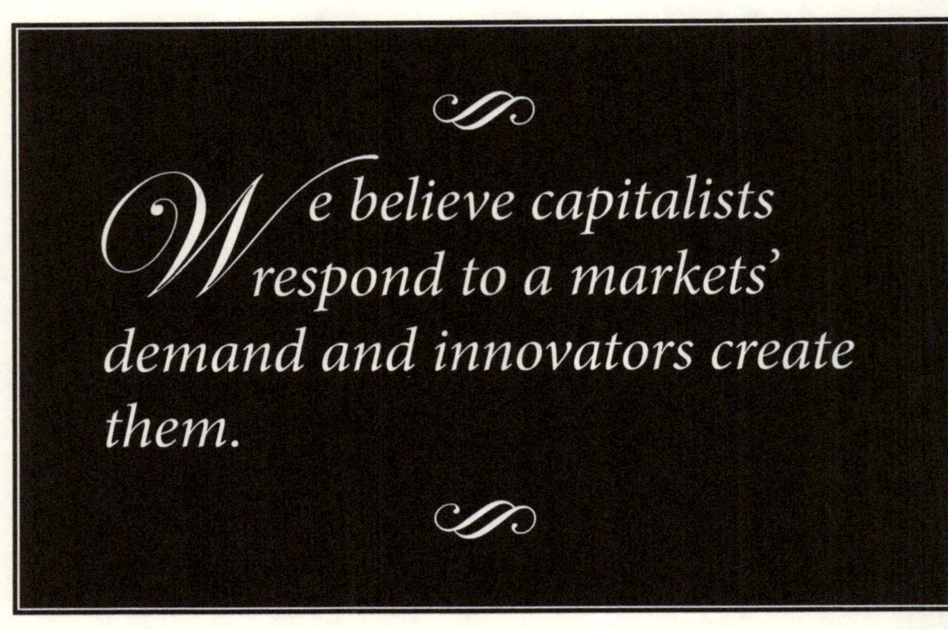

We believe capitalists respond to a markets' demand and innovators create them.

Journal your initial thoughts below:

Belief Journal

1. If you do not agree, create a belief statement using your own words. If you do agree, feel free to put this belief into your own words.

2. Did this belief come from your own experiences or from some else's beliefs? Explain.

3. What values will guide your actions in living out this belief?

"All the great ages have been ages of belief."
- Ralph Waldo Emerson

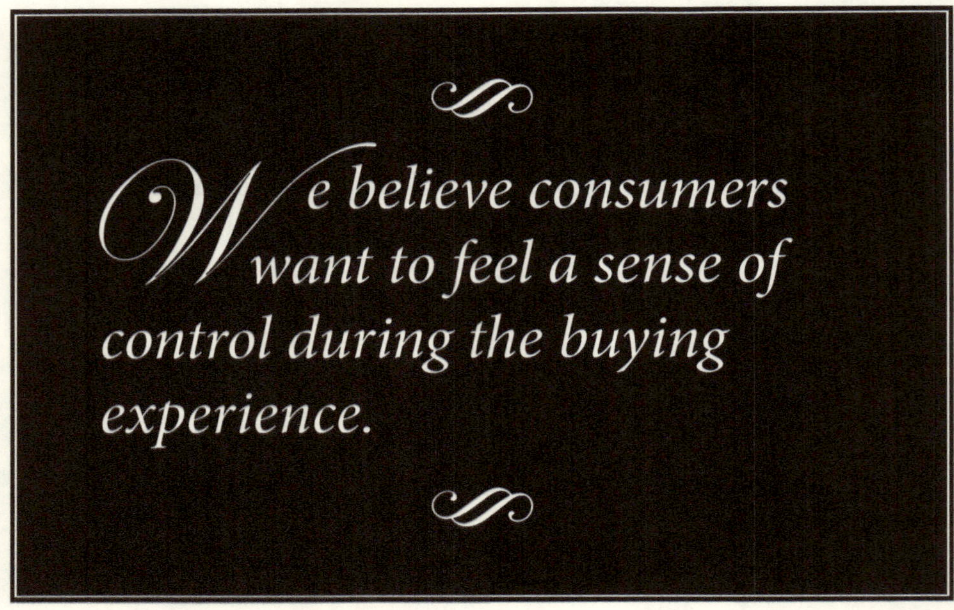

Journal your initial thoughts below:

Belief Journal

1. If you do not agree, create a belief statement using your own words. If you do agree, feel free to put this belief into your own words.

2. Did this belief come from your own experiences or from some else's beliefs? Explain.

3. What values will guide your actions in living out this belief?

"All personal breakthroughs begin with a change in beliefs."
- Anthony Robbins

WALT DISNEY

Walt Disney is a shining example of transferred beliefs. Known as one of the greatest innovators of our time, Walt Disney operated by a deep set of beliefs he formed while watching his father struggle to obtain his dreams.

Legend has it that Walt Disney explained his success with the following statement; "I dream, I test my dreams against my beliefs, I dare to take risks, and I execute my vision to make those dreams come true." It is believed that from this statement a mantra was formed that drove everything Walt Disney did: Dream, Believe, Dare, Do.

Behind Disney's mantra lies the core beliefs of honesty, reliability, loyalty, and respect for people as individuals. The Disney companies would translate these deep beliefs and mantra into the ten management principles/values that remain in practice to this day.

Core Beliefs

1. Make Everyone's Dreams Come True: Enables members of the organization to dream and develop their creative talents.
2. You Better Believe It: Ensures members possess a clear understanding of the company beliefs.
3. Never a Customer, Always a Guest: Handle everyone as a guest that deserves respect and honesty.
4. All for One and One for All: Teamwork that fosters intense loyalty, enthusiasm and commitment.
5. Share the Spotlight: Emphasizes the importance of partnering with other like-minded organizations.
6. Dare to Dare: Encourages risk-taking as a method of cultivating innovative ideas.
7. Practice, Practice, Practice: Emphasizes the importance on training that leads to habits.
8. Make Your Elephant Fly: Long-term vision must be aligned with short-term execution.
9. Capture the Magic with Storyboards: Generating solutions through enhanced communications.
10. Give Details Top Billing: Balancing a quest for perfection with the bottom line by measuring results to ensure the effort matches the outcome.

Accomplishments

The following is a timeline of the roles Walt Disney played and accomplishments that have been attributed to his ventures. How many of the corporate values were formed from his experiences surrounding what he believed? Identify some experiences in the timeline that may have shaped the corporate values.

1919 After driving an ambulance through Europe, Walt returns to the US, moves to Kansas City and gets a job at the Posman-Rubin Commercial Art Studio.

1920 Walt meets Ub Iwerks, together they form Iwerks-Disney Commercial Artists.

Walt & Ub work for the Kansas City Slide Company.

Walt names the films "Laugh-O-grams."

1922 Walt incorporates "Laugh-O-gram Films" with $15,000 from local investors.

1923 Walt moves to Hollywood planning to become a director. Roy (Walt's brother) was already in California.

Walt & Roy sign a contract with M.J. Winkler, a New York cartoon distributor.

1924 Walt hires the first animator, Rollin Hamilton and moves into a small store with a window bearing "Disney Bros. Studio."

The first *Alice Comedies* reaches theaters.

Ub Iwerks moves to California to join Disney Productions.

Walt invites Hugh Harmen & Rudy Ising to work for him.

1926 Walt renames the studio to the "Walt Disney Studio."

1927 Walt Disney Studios is authorized to make *Oswald the Lucky Rabbit* series. All rights were sold to Mintz distribution.

1928 Walt develops Mickey Mouse and along with Ub Iwerks creates a new cartoon, *Plane Crazy*. Audiences were in love with the mouse.

Steamboat Willie, the third cartoon is created.

Walt pursues New York film companies to record the cartoon with sound.

Walt urges Ub to go forward with the fourth Mickey Mouse Cartoon *The Barn Dance*.

Steamboat Willie opens while billed as "the first animated cartoon with sound."

Film companies come calling for Walt to make a deal.

A deal with Pat Powers, who wants to promote Cinephone, is struck.

1929 Walt plans to release *Skeleton Dance* as the 1st of a new series of cartoons called Silly Symphonies. This new film was also released in Technicolor, a brand new color technique, that Walt Disney held rights to for two years.

Mickey Mouse turns into a national craze.

Mickey Mouse Clubs spring up all over the country.

1930 Walt starts anew breaking off negotiations with Pat Powers, suspecting him of being crooked.

Columbia Pictures signs with Disney, as Walt breaks all ties with Powers.

Roy Disney signs the first contract for merchandising.

Walt assigns Ub Iwerks to devise a comic strip.

Syndication comes from King Features and Mickey Mouse makes his first comic strip.

Pluto makes 1st appearance in a Mickey Mouse cartoon, *The Chain Gang.*

1931 The Mickey Mouse Clubs reach a million members.

Mickey Mouse is now known in every civilized country.

1932 Goofy makes 1st appearance in *Mickey's Revue.*

Herman Kamen signs a contract to represent the Walt Disney Studios. He licenses Lionel Corporation for merchandising Mickey and Minnie toy trains.

The association with Disney is credited for the return of Lionel during the depression.

Walt agrees to United Artists' proposal.

United Artists agrees to grant Disney 2 years exclusive use of 3-color Technicolor.

The first class of the Disney Art School is held at the Chouinard Art Institue.

1933 *Three Little Pigs*, the 36th Silly Symphony, is produced. Audiences everywhere love it and relate it to the people vs. the Depression. "Who's Afraid of the Big Bad Wolf" becomes a national rally cry.

Roy convinces Walt to produce 3 more "Pig" movies.

1934-36 Donald Duck debut's in a Silly Symphony film, *The Wise Little Hen.*

Walt's staff grows to 187 employees.

Walt announces that *Snow White and the Seven Dwarfs* will be the 1st feature film.

Disneys disassociate themselves with United Artists.

Disneys sign a releasing agreement for shorts and for *Snow White* with RKO.

1937-38 Donald Duck gets his own series of short films.

Snow White and the Seven Dwarfs debuts and wins an Academy Award.

The Disney Studios are expanded and they put deposit down on property in Burbank, CA.

Work begins on a second feature, *Pinocchio.*

Walt decides that Mickey Mouse should star in a feature of *The Sorcerer's Apprentice.*

Leopold Stokwski volunteers to conduct the music. Stokowski tells Disney to create a single Feature - *Fantasia.*

Bambi is started at the same time but is last to be released due to the time it took to draw the animals.

1939 Burbank Studio construction continues, making it a workers paradise.

The start of World War II causes business of *Pinocchio* to fall short of what is expected.

1940 *Fantasia* opens at New York's Broadway Theater (formally called "The Colony").

Disney offers public stock, 600,000 shares of common stock sold at $5 a piece. Sold out.

Disney employees grow to 1,000 workers.

Dumbo is produced and finished in 1 year.

Ub Iwerks returns to the Walt Disney Studios.

1941 Walt makes a film during a goodwill tour of South America.

Saludos Amigos and *The Three Caballeros* are the result of the South America trip. Both films are successful in North & South America.

High demand for war films occurs.

The army moves into the Disney Studios.

1942 *Bambi* is released.

1946 *Make Mine Music*, a short cartoon, is released.

The work on *Mickey And The Beanstalk*, interrupted due to the war, is resumed.

Song of the South is produced and premieres in Atlanta.

"Zip-A-Dee-Doo-Dah" wins best movie song by the Academy of Motion Picture Arts & Sciences, while James Baskett, who plays Uncle Remus, wins an Oscar.

1947 Walt films Alaska suggesting a feature length film based on the life of seals. The film wins an Academy Award for best 2-reel documentary.

Walt assigns all of his top talent to make *Cinderella*, *Peter Pan*, and *Alice in Wonderland*.

Walt begins plans in August to build an amusement area to be named Mickey Mouse Park.

1949 The Walt Disney Music Company is formed.

1950 *Cinderella* debuts as the first hit for Disney Studios since *Snow White and the Seven Dwarfs*.

1951 Walt schedules *Alice In Wonderland* to follow *Cinderella*.

Peter Pan was the next cartoon in production.

Walt agrees to produce a Christmas show for NBC, attracting a huge audience.

1952 Script production begins on *Lady and the Tramp*.

The Sword and the Rose and *Rob Roy* are produced.

Walt contemplates *20,000 Leagues Under the Sea*, a Jules Verne classic adventure.

Fearful RKO couldn't sell the film *The Living Desert*, Roy establishes Buena Vista.

Disney films thereafter are distributed by Buena Vista.

1953 Walt's vision of an amusement park begins, naming it Disneyland.

Walt creates WED Enterprises to organize the project.

Walt and Herb Ryman draw out the plans for the park in one weekend.

Roy Disney & Leonard Goldman come to an agreement with ABC.

Disney's first "Adventures in Music" animated film, *Melody*, is released. The film was made in 3-D, the first such film to be released in the US.

Walt commissions the Stanford Research Institute to find the ideal location for Disneyland. Anaheim, California is selected as the location for Disneyland.

1954 *Davy Crockett* is the hit of the inaugural Disneyland season and "The Ballad of Davy Crockett" is #1 on the charts for 13 weeks.

Walt buys 244 acres of land near Anaheim, California, as the site for his theme park.

Plans for Disneyland park and TV show are announced.

The television series opens with "The Disneyland Story" describing coming attractions of the park and TV show.

1955 Walt Disney releases the film, *Lady and the Tramp* in the US through Buena Vista. It is the first cartoon feature to be filmed in CinemaScope and processed in Technicolor.

The Santa Fe and Disneyland Railway makes its first trip around the park fulfilling the wish of a boy with leukemia.

By December Disneyland welcomes its one millionth visitor.

Disneyland television series opens its second season on ABC with *Dumbo.*

Walt introduces "The Mickey Mouse Club" program.

1956 *Sleeping Beauty* is put into production.

Walt's main focus is on Disneyland, live-action films and television.

The Disneyland Hotel opens, on a 60-acre site next to Disneyland.

1957 Disney introduces a third television series named "Zorro", an adventure on the ABC network.

Bambi is re-released in theaters and is a success.

The live-action film, *Old Yeller* is released.

1958 *The Shaggy Dog* is released and is a surprising success.

Disneyland's Columbia ship is christened.

1959 The Matterhorn, a bobsled-racing ride, is opened, as well as the Submarine Voyage and the Disneyland-Alweg Monorail System.

A Motor Boat cruise and a revamp of the Autopia is also opened.

The E-Ticket is introduced.

1960 *Pollyana* is released.

1961 Walt Disney's "Wonderful World of Color" makes its debut on NBC with a new character, Ludwig Von Drake.

1963 Enchanted Tiki Room opens at Disneyland. Audio-Animatronics is developed by WED.

1964 *Mary Poppins* premieres at Grauman's Chinese Theater in Hollywood and gets rave reviews.

Mary Poppins is nominated for 13 Academy Awards.

President Johnson presents Walt with the Medal of Freedom at the White House.

1965 Walt Disney sends his brother, Roy, and a few other Disney executives to Florida, to purchase land for a Community of Tomorrow.

1966 Walt Disney is the Grand Marshall for the Tournament of Roses Parade, in Pasadena California.

The "New Orleans Square" area opens at Disneyland.

Walt announces plans for an Experimental Prototype Community of Tomorrow, EPCOT.

Walt Disney cultivated such a strong vision, and a belief system that supported it, that 45 years later his vision is still being fulfilled. How strong is your vision and the beliefs that drive it? Are you sharing your beliefs and vision with others in a manor that inspires their adoption? Do the people you surrounded yourself with compliment your beliefs?

Let's continue our journey so you may discover the answers to these questions . . .

Awaken Your Opportunities

relationship beliefs

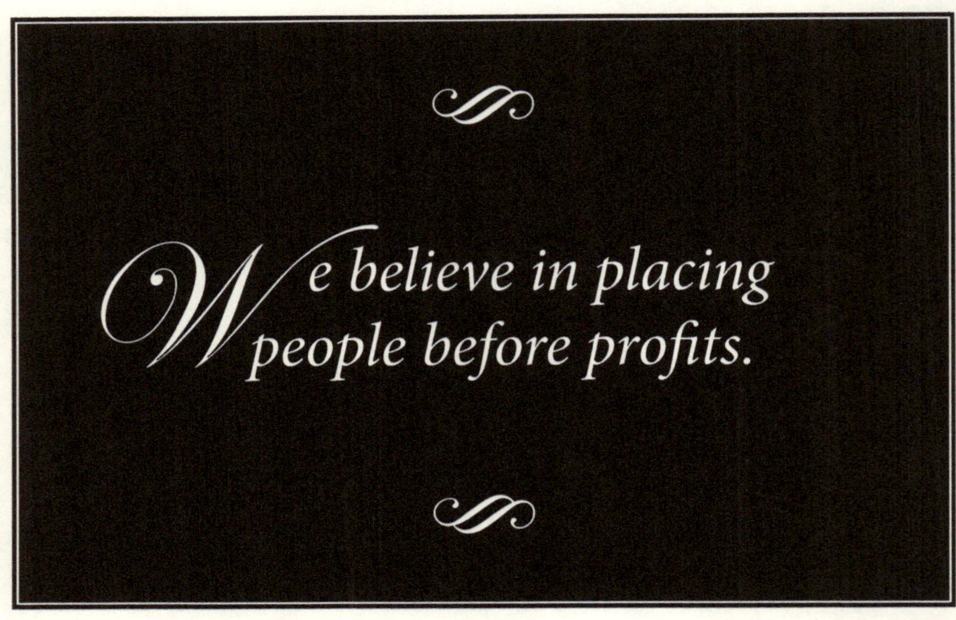

Journal your initial thoughts below:

Belief Journal

1. **If you do not agree, create a belief statement using your own words. If you do agree, feel free to put this belief into your own words.**

2. **Did this belief come from your own experiences or from some else's beliefs? Explain.**

3. **What values will guide your actions in living out this belief?**

"He does not believe that does not live according to his belief."
- Thomas Fuller M.D.

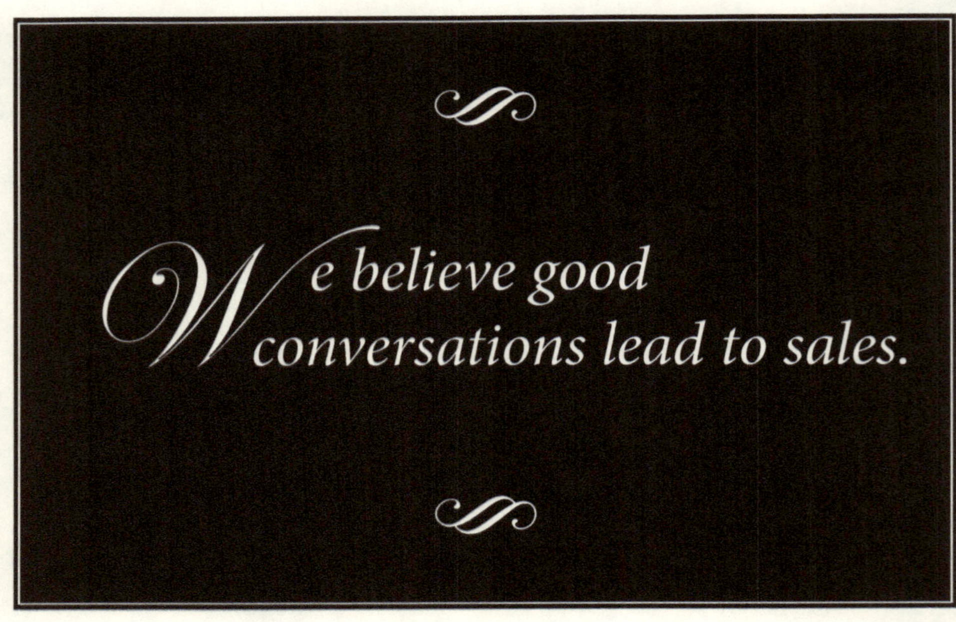

Journal your initial thoughts below:

Belief Journal

1. If you do not agree, create a belief statement using your own words. If you do agree, feel free to put this belief into your own words.

2. Did this belief come from your own experiences or from some else's beliefs? Explain.

3. What values will guide your actions in living out this belief?

"Many a time I have wanted to stop talking and find out what I really believed."
- Walter Lippmann

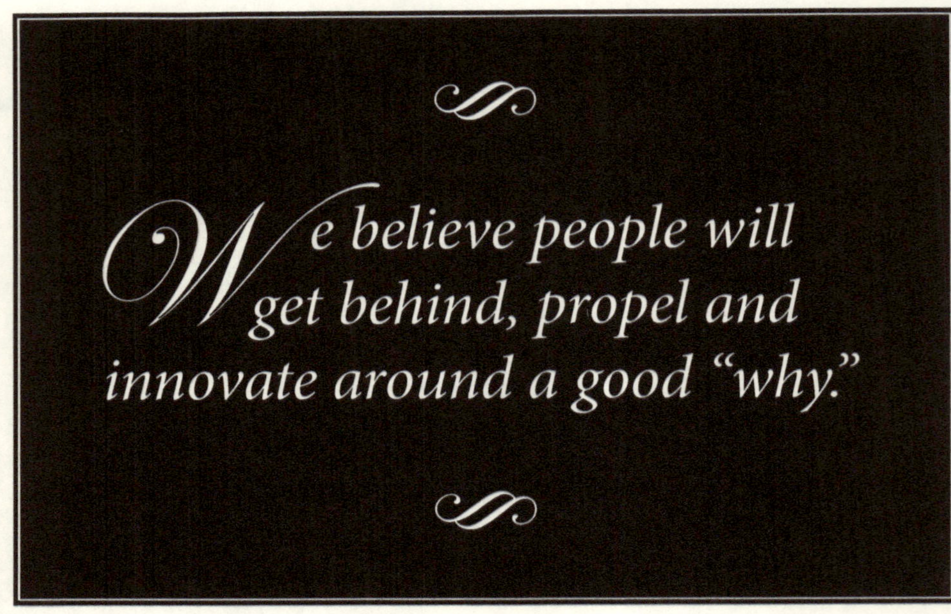
We believe people will get behind, propel and innovate around a good "why."

Journal your initial thoughts below:

Belief Journal

1. **If you do not agree, create a belief statement using your own words. If you do agree, feel free to put this belief into your own words.**

2. **Did this belief come from your own experiences or from some else's beliefs? Explain.**

3. **What values will guide your actions in living out this belief?**

"One person with a belief is equal to a force of ninety-nine who have only interests."
- John Stuart Mill

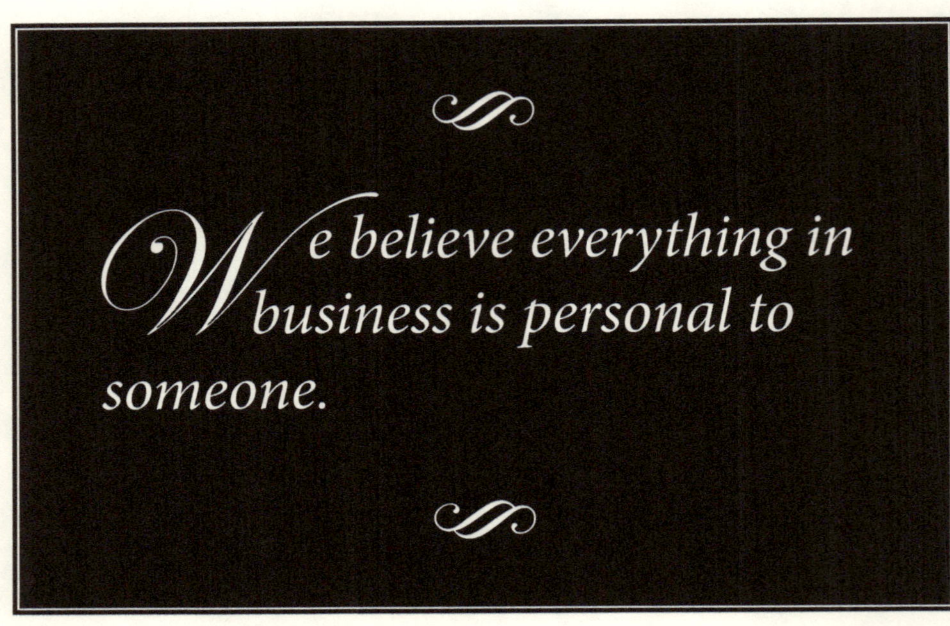

Journal your initial thoughts below:

Belief Journal

1. If you do not agree, create a belief statement using your own words. If you do agree, feel free to put this belief into your own words.

2. Did this belief come from your own experiences or from some else's beliefs? Explain.

3. What values will guide your actions in living out this belief?

"Only a real risk tests the reality of a belief."
- C.S. Lewis

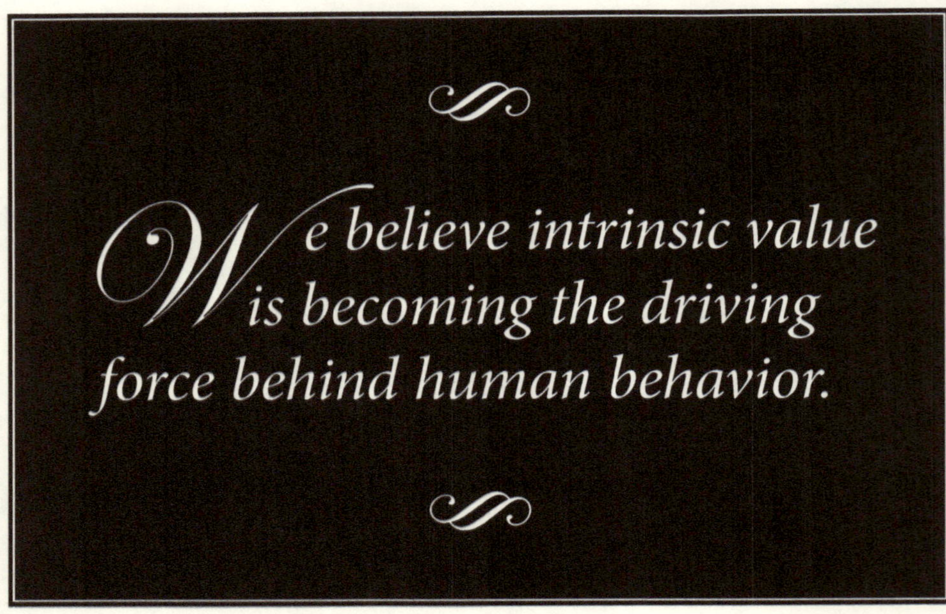
We believe intrinsic value is becoming the driving force behind human behavior.

Journal your initial thoughts below:

Belief Journal

1. If you do not agree, create a belief statement using your own words. If you do agree, feel free to put this belief into your own words.

2. Did this belief come from your own experiences or from some else's beliefs? Explain.

3. What values will guide your actions in living out this belief?

"Strong beliefs win strong men, and then make them stronger."
- Walter Bagehot

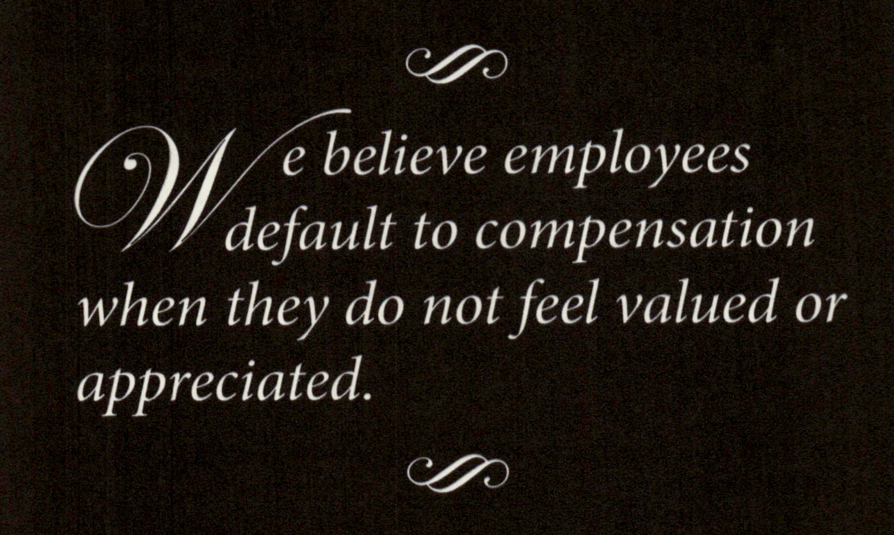
We believe employees default to compensation when they do not feel valued or appreciated.

Journal your initial thoughts below:

Belief Journal

1. If you do not agree, create a belief statement using your own words. If you do agree, feel free to put this belief into your own words.

2. Did this belief come from your own experiences or from some else's beliefs? Explain.

3. What values will guide your actions in living out this belief?

"Realizing that our actions, feelings and behaviour are the result of our own images and beliefs gives us the level that psychology has always needed for changing personality."
- Maxwell Maltz

We believe clear expectations and accountability is replacing task delegation and micro-management.

Journal your initial thoughts below:

Belief Journal

1. If you do not agree, create a belief statement using your own words. If you do agree, feel free to put this belief into your own words.

2. Did this belief come from your own experiences or from some else's beliefs? Explain.

3. What values will guide your actions in living out this belief?

"Whether you believe you can, or you can't, you are right."
- Henry Ford

ZAPPOS

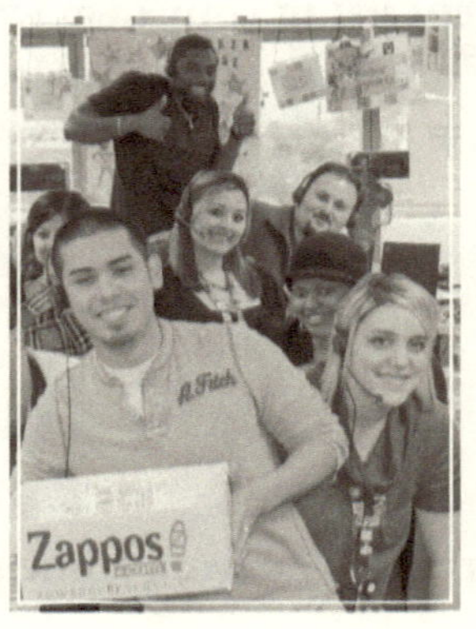

Zappos is a shining example of collective beliefs. Nick Swinmurn found inspiration through the frustration of not being able to find a pair of brown Airwalks at his local mall. His frustration spurred an idea to sell shoes online. Swinmurn approached Tony Hsieh and Alfred Lin with the idea. Swinmurn, Hsieh, and Lin had a strong belief that great customer service and a fantastic buying experience was the core to success in today's society.

As Zappos began growing around this belief, they needed a set of values that would guide everyone in the company to consistently produce a fantastic customer experience. Tony Hsieh engaged all the employees, challenging them to weigh in on what values the company should live by. A year later, the following list was finalized, and it has been driving Zappos' monumental success over the past 10 years.

Zappos 10 Core Values

1. Deliver Wow Through Service
2. Embrace And Drive Change
3. Create Fun And A Little Weirdness
4. Be Adventurous, Creative And Open-Minded
5. Pursue Growth And Learning
6. Build Open And Honest Relationships With Communication
7. Build A Positive Team And Family Spirit
8. Do More With Less
9. Be Passionate And Determined
10. Be Humble

Accomplishment(s)

The following is a timeline of events and accomplishments that have been attributed to Zappos. Notice that they experience very little adversity as they grow at a staggering rate. Which fueled their growth: beliefs or an ability to crunch numbers?

1999 Founder Nick Swinmurn comes up with the idea to start an online shoe destination called ShoeSite.com.

Swinmurn meets Tony Hsieh, a young entrepreneur who invests $500,000 in the company.

In July, the name is changed to Zappos.com, after "zapatos", which is Spanish for "shoes."

Gross sales are minimal.

2000 Hsieh, then running a venture capital firm called Venture Frogs, comes on board as co-CEO with Swinmurn.

$1.6 million in gross sales.

2001 $8.6 million in gross sales.

2002 Zappos takes on its own inventory, opening a fulfillment center in Kentucky.

$32 million in gross sales.

2003 $70 million in gross sales.

2004 Zappos moves from San Francisco to its current location in Henderson, Nevada.

Sequoia Capital invests in the site.

The first Zappos outlet store opens in Kentucky.

The company publishes its first Culture Book, filled with employee contributions about the corporate culture.

$184 million in gross sales.

2005 Hsieh hires Venture Frogs co-founder Alfred Lin to be the e-tailer's CFO full-time.

Sequoia provides a second round of investment, totaling $35 million altogether.

Zappos offers its first quit-now bonuses ($100 at the time) to new hires that want to leave after training. It is now $2,000. Footwear News names Zappos E-tailer of the Year.

$370 million in gross sales.

2006 Swinmurn leaves the company. Zappos moves to a larger fulfillment center in Shepherdsville, KY.

$597 million in gross sales.

2007 Zappos' Canadian site launches.

The company acquires footwear and accessories e-tailer 6pm.com from eBags.com.

New categories are added, including handbags, eyewear, clothing, kids' merchandise and watches.

$840 million in gross sales.

2008 $1 billion in gross sales.

Zappos debuts first TV ad campaign, "Put a Little Zappos in Your Day."

In July, the fulfillment center in Shepherdsville installs a new system using Kiva robots to help fill orders.

In November, Zappos lays off 8 percent of its workforce.

In December, the company launches ZapposInsights.com, a subscription service ($40 per month), where other businesses learn from its success and pose questions to current employees.

2009 Zappos turns 10.

In February, Fortune magazine ranks Zappos as No. 23 on its "100 Best Companies to Work For" list.

Product-driven ads hit major cable networks.

In July of 2009, Zappos.com, Inc. announced its plans to join the Amazon.com, Inc. family. A strong passion for customer service aligned both companies. By 2010, Zappos.com, Inc's growth caused a need for corporate restructure in order to continue to offer customers the very best service possible.

What is your business' growth potential with the right beliefs?

Awaken Your Connections

attraction beliefs

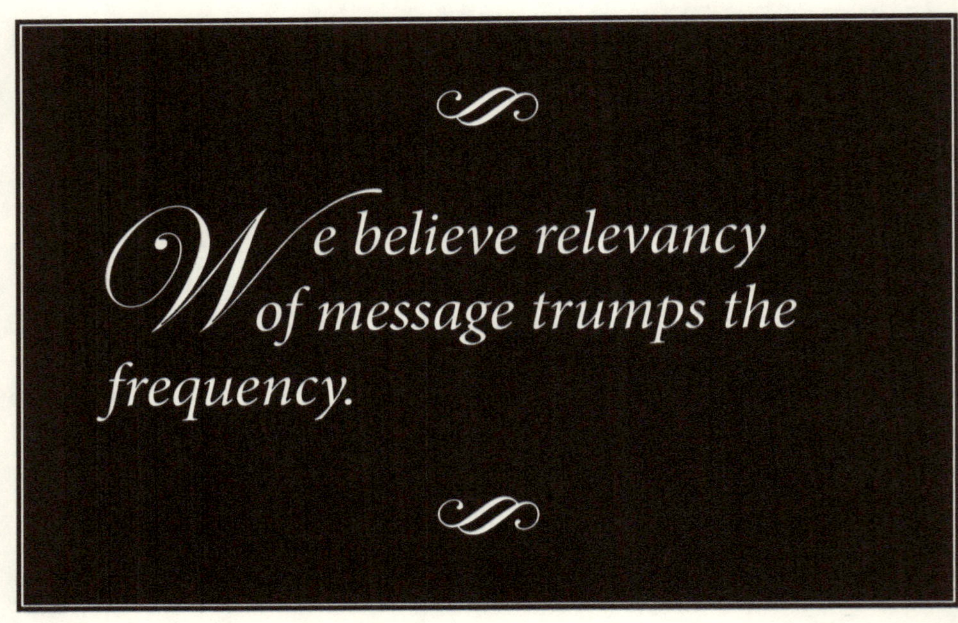
We believe relevancy of message trumps the frequency.

Journal your initial thoughts below:

Belief Journal

1. If you do not agree, create a belief statement using your own words. If you do agree, feel free to put this belief into your own words.

2. Did this belief come from your own experiences or from some else's beliefs? Explain.

3. What values will guide your actions in living out this belief?

"Absurdity, n.: A statement or belief manifestly inconsistent with one's own opinion".
- Ambrose Bierce

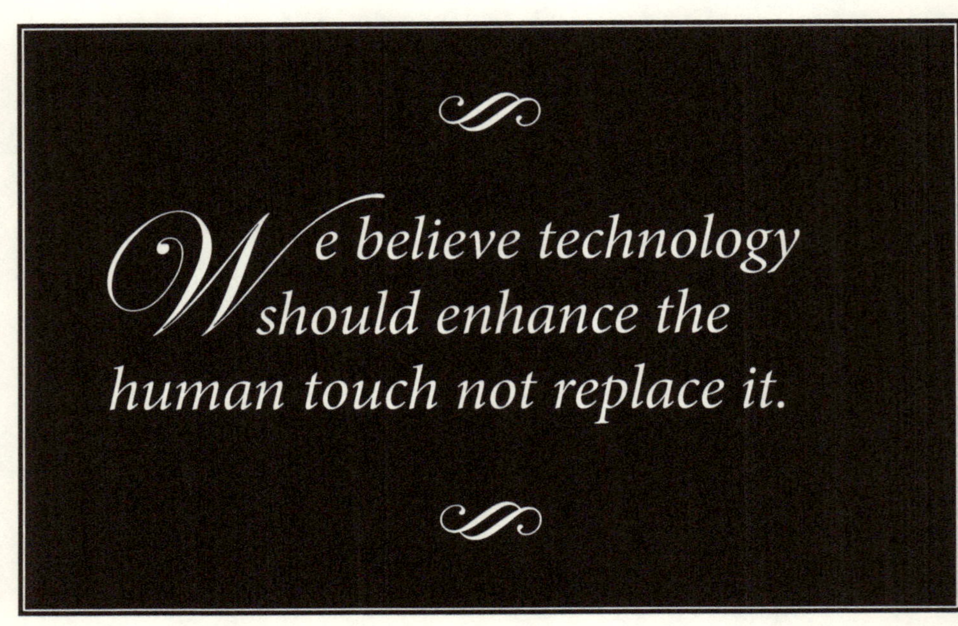
We believe technology should enhance the human touch not replace it.

Journal your initial thoughts below:

Belief Journal

1. If you do not agree, create a belief statement using your own words. If you do agree, feel free to put this belief into your own words.

2. Did this belief come from your own experiences or from some else's beliefs? Explain.

3. What values will guide your actions in living out this belief?

"It is from numberless diverse acts of courage and belief that human history is shaped. Each time a man stands up for an ideal, or acts to improve the lot of others, or strikes out against injustice, he sends forth a tiny ripple of hope."
- Robert F. Kennedy

We believe good communication begins with understanding the other person's perspective.

Journal your initial thoughts below:

Belief Journal

1. If you do not agree, create a belief statement using your own words. If you do agree, feel free to put this belief into your own words.

2. Did this belief come from your own experiences or from some else's beliefs? Explain.

3. What values will guide your actions in living out this belief?

"If you must tell me your opinions, tell me what you believe in.
I have plenty of doubts of my own."
- Johann Wolfgang von Goethe

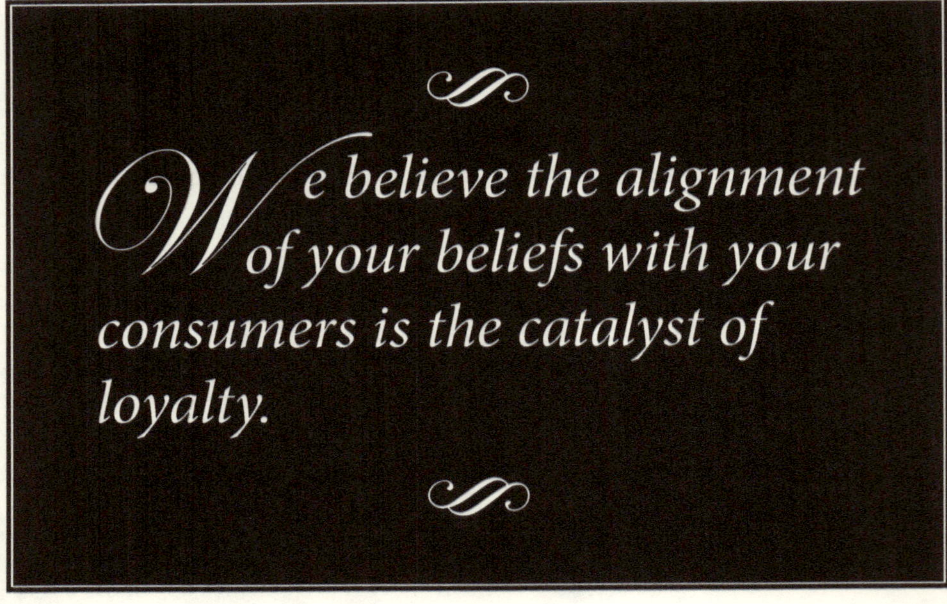

We believe the alignment of your beliefs with your consumers is the catalyst of loyalty.

Journal your initial thoughts below:

Belief Journal

1. If you do not agree, create a belief statement using your own words. If you do agree, feel free to put this belief into your own words.

2. Did this belief come from your own experiences or from some else's beliefs? Explain.

3. What values will guide your actions in living out this belief?

"The world we see that seems so insane is the result of a belief system that is not working. To perceive the world differently, we must be willing to change our belief system, let the past slip away, expand our sense of now, and dissolve the fear in our minds."
- William James

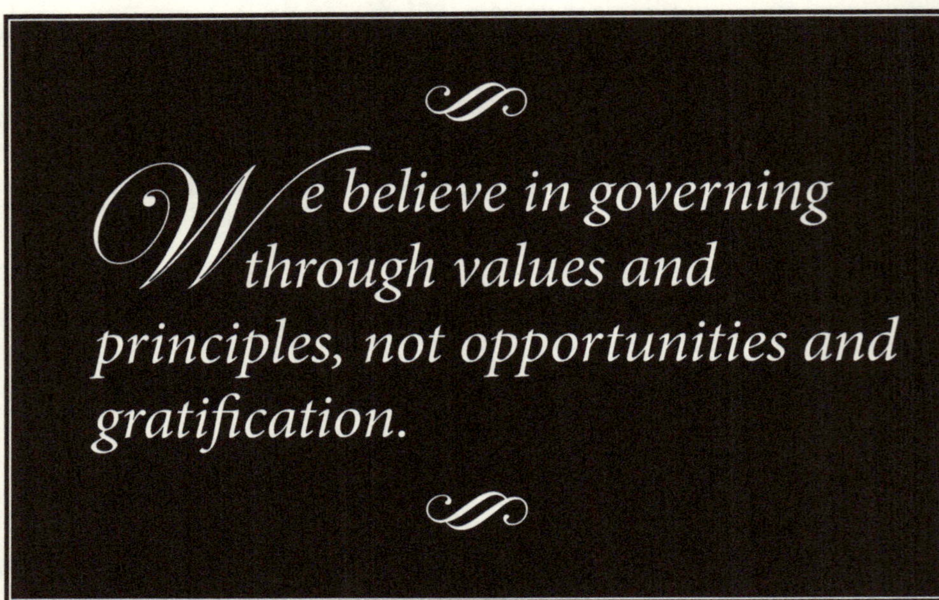
We believe in governing through values and principles, not opportunities and gratification.

Journal your initial thoughts below:

Belief Journal

1. If you do not agree, create a belief statement using your own words. If you do agree, feel free to put this belief into your own words.

2. Did this belief come from your own experiences or from some else's beliefs? Explain.

3. What values will guide your actions in living out this belief?

"The eloquent man is he who is no eloquent speaker, but who is inwardly drunk with a certain belief."
- Ralph Waldo Emerson

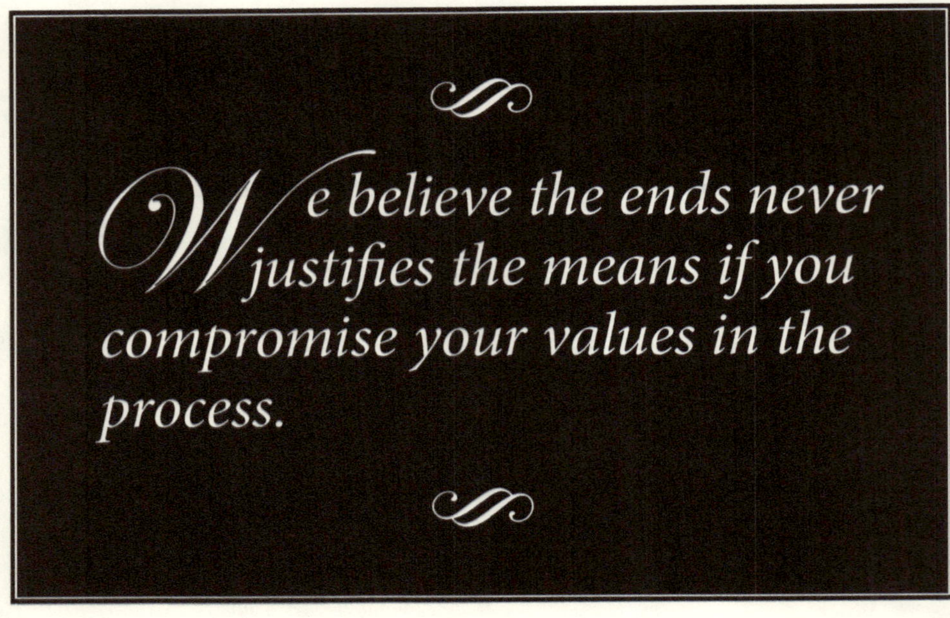

We believe the ends never justifies the means if you compromise your values in the process.

Journal your initial thoughts below:

Belief Journal

1. If you do not agree, create a belief statement using your own words. If you do agree, feel free to put this belief into your own words.

2. Did this belief come from your own experiences or from some else's beliefs? Explain.

3. What values will guide your actions in living out this belief?

"Man is made by his belief. As he believes, so he is."
- Johann Wolfgang von Goethe

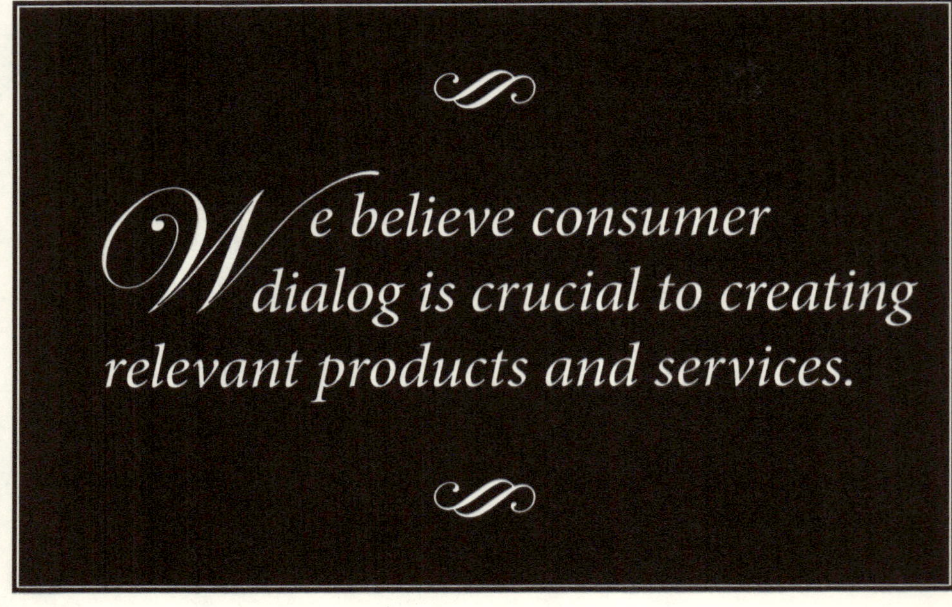
We believe consumer dialog is crucial to creating relevant products and services.

Journal your initial thoughts below:

Belief Journal

1. If you do not agree, create a belief statement using your own words. If you do agree, feel free to put this belief into your own words.

2. Did this belief come from your own experiences or from some else's beliefs? Explain.

3. What values will guide your actions in living out this belief?

"Our belief was that if we kept putting great products in front of customers, they would continue to open their wallets."
- Steve Jobs

Conclusion

Congratulations! You have completed a journey that few will. The question is: "What are you going to do now?" Most people revert to what's familiar because it is safe, comfortable, and requires little effort. Experiences bestow new knowledge on us, changing our perspectives. What we do with this knowledge is the difference between simply gaining information and personal transformation. Robert Frost understood this and wrote about it in his famous poem, "The Road Not Taken," when he chose the road less traveled. I believe our Maker gave us the capacity to be great. Still, few have the courage to shed all the false perceptions society has ingrained in us, diminishing our worth.

If you stop the experience here, you will only have gained a new perspective and nothing more! But, if you choose to take action on what you have discovered, then the outlines below will guide you in creating your own manifesto.

This manifesto will be your tool for transformation, consisting of your beliefs and values. You'll use it to guide your actions, measure areas to improve and, if applicable, create the culture that drives growth. If you want to create a lasting transformation, begin sharing this experience and your manifesto with others. Once you declare it to others then the law of natural accountability takes hold. In other words, there's no turning back. Are you ready to take the road less traveled?

Personal & Partner Outline to Create Your Culture Manifesto(s):

- ❏ Create a list of all your beliefs and the corresponding value for each.
- ❏ Consolidate repeat values.
- ❏ Write a short description of what each value means to you.
- ❏ Finalize your list of beliefs and values with their descriptions.
- ❏ Display in whatever format will help you live by it daily (plaque, notebook, screensaver, etc.).

Startup, Department & Company Outline to Create Your Culture Manifesto:

Each participant:

- ❏ Create a list of all your beliefs and the corresponding value for each.
- ❏ Consolidate repeat values.
- ❏ Write a short description of what each value means to you.
- ❏ Finalize your list of beliefs and values with their descriptions.

Group exercises:

- ❏ Conduct synergy meeting(s) where each participant brings their finalized list.
- ❏ Display someone's list as a baseline for all to see and let the synergy begin.
- ❏ Finalize your groups' list of beliefs and values with their descriptions.
- ❏ Display in whatever format will help you live by it daily (plaque, notebook, screensaver, etc.).

Afterword

Over the last 20 years, I have worked with hundreds of startups, small businesses, and organizations to help them better connect with their consumers. Most of them don't know who they really are as a person, a department, and/or a company. Few truly understand the environment that they are doing business in. Few truly know whom they serve and, more importantly, how they serve them. Few truly know how to connect with their consumers on a level that is authentic and creates loyalty. Why?

Well, the answer is simple. Selfishness. They believe that the primary reason to start a business is to serve their own needs. We have been programmed to think the measurement of our success is directly linked to the bottom line and that the one with the most stuff wins. Now, I enjoy stuff as much as the next person, but it does not define my level of success anymore. When I first started my business career, I was all about status and stuff as a measure of my success. This one belief sabotaged me over and over and over again.

Sustainable success, however, is rooted in living what you believe and, as an entrepreneur, transforming those beliefs into a way to serve others. The starting point is discovering what we believe. One of my favorite companies doing this is Toms Shoes. Their one-for-one model is changing the world. For every pair of shoes that are purchased, Toms donates a pair of shoes to an impoverished area of the world. Having already given away more than one million pairs of shoes, they are one of the few companies that are accomplishing things far greater than just a healthy bottom line.

As individuals, we are powerful, yet we shrink in our efforts. We often confuse this for acting humble or being a team player. By illustrating our power in a truly humble way, we can inspire others to do the same. Combining our power with others unlocks infinite ways to impact the world. When was the last time you inspired someone in business? If you did, do you remember how it felt? How would you like to feel that way almost all the time? Wouldn't it be magnificent? You can! It all starts with your beliefs.

It is important to start an internal and external dialog that challenges people to understand, change, and solidify their beliefs. *Awaken* is a tool designed to help you start your journey to true empowerment. My hope is that *Awaken* will spur a national discussion on the heart of American businesses and what we need to do to replace greed with service. Please go to *www.facebook.com/awakenbook* and join the discussion. We want to hear your beliefs, ideas, and causes that may play a role in determining how business is done in America. I pray this "thought book" has helped to equip you to become who you were designed to be.

GamePlan Mentoring Solutions empowers entrepreneurs to create the companies others care about. Most companies are formed with good intentions to fulfill a need or desire, but their actions are motivated by profits. Today's consumer sees right through this and wants to know why they should buy from you versus your competition. GamePlan guides entrepreneurs to discover who they truly are, why their organization really matters, and how to authentically connect with the people they serve in a way that generates sales, loyalty, and repeat business.

GamePlan creates solutions focused on causes, concepts, cultures and connections that empower entrepreneurs to obtain their goals.

We at GamePlan are excited to present *Awaken*. This is the first step toward developing an understanding of how to achieve your goals as a person, a department, and an organization.

To order *Awaken* in bulk, connect with us at:
www.awakenmybeliefs.com

If you wish to learn more about our other
products/services connect with us at:
www.gameplanmentoring.com

Endnotes

Wikipedia:

http://en.wikipedia.org/wiki/Benjamin_Franklin

http://en.wikipedia.org/wiki/Walt_Disney

http://en.wikipedia.org/wiki/Zappos.com

Books:

Franklin, Benjamin. Mémoires de la vie privée de Benjamin Franklin. Buisson, Paris: 1791.

Capodagli, Bill and Jackson, Lynn. The Disney Way: Harnessing the Management Secrets of Disney in Your Company. New York: McGraw-Hill Book Co., 2006.

Internet:

http://www.foundationsmag.com/civility.html

http://www.zappos.com

http://fi.edu/franklin/timeline/timeline.html

http://www.benfranklin300.org/etc_timeline.htm

http://www.justdisney.com/walt_disney/timeline/

http://www.drakkar91.com/disney/wdwtime.htm

http://www.ideafinder.com/history/inventors/disney.htm

http://www.buzzle.com/articles/timeline-of-walt-disney-life-history-of-walt-disney.html

http://about.zappos.com/press-center/media-coverage/zappos-milestone-timeline

http://maaw.info/ArticleSummaries/ArtSumCapodagliJackson99.htm

http://www.inc.com/magazine/20060901/hidi-hsieh.html

http://blogs.hbr.org/cs/2010/05/how_zappos_infuses_culture_using_core_values.html

http://www.successmagazine.com/the-business-of-giving/PARAMS/article/852

http://en.wikipedia.org/wiki/TOMS_Shoes

http://about.zappos.com/press-center/media-kit

http://www.loc.gov/pictures/item/2004671903/

http://simple.wikipedia.org/wiki/File:Walt_Disney_NYWTS.jpg

ABOUT THE AUTHOR

Scott Cutcher is the co-founder of GamePlan Mentoring Solutions, a pioneering company devoted to transforming the heart of American business. A native of Piqua, Ohio, he now calls Nashville, Tennessee his home along with his wife Cindy and their source of joy, Lydia.

You can reach Scott with feedback or to discuss speaking engagements at: scott@gameplanmentoring.com

ABOUT THE AUTHOR'S BUSINESS PARTNER:

Steven Lowry is the co-founder of GamePlan Mentoring Solutions, a pioneering company devoted to transforming the heart of American business. A native of Kokomo, Indiana, he now calls Nashville, Tennessee home along with his wife Kelly and their adorable dog, Belle.

You can reach Steven with feedback at: steven@gameplanmentoring.com

Special thanks to Everett Laster who convinced this story teller to take the first leap in becoming an author.

www.ingramcontent.com/pod-product-compliance
Lightning Source LLC
Chambersburg PA
CBHW022019170526
45157CB00003B/1285

* 9 7 8 1 2 5 7 9 5 9 1 6 7 *